A Five Hundred Pound Amoeba

and Other Psychiatric Tales

Steve Sobel, M.D.

An earlier version of "A Song for Kevin" (entitled "A Song for Me") was published in *Hektoen International Journal of Medical Humanities* (2011).

Earlier versions of "Just in Case" (2012) and "Messages from an Ex and/or Current Girlfriend" (2011) were published in *Yale Journal for Medical Humanities*.

An earlier version of "Seasonal Acrophobia" was published in *Cell 2 Soul: The Humane Health Care Blog* (2007).

To my family and friends whose advice and encouragement

convinced me to persevere in this endeavor.

The following stories are fictional. The characters depicted are not

based on any actual people. Although their stories are consistent

with the reality I encounter as a psychiatrist, they are purely

creations of my imagination.

CONTENTS

A Five Hundred Pound Amoeba

Through the gloomy fog, his wife's plaintive voice floated to Jake's desolate hideout.

"Jake, you have to get up! You can't lie there forever. At least take a shower today. I'm really getting worried about you. This has gone way too far!"

Eons passed before Jake deciphered Leah's words. Judging by the muffled, garbled nature of her speech, he initially suspected he must be underwater, before remembering it was his own brain that had become flooded with some noxious, viscous substance. He recognized there was an urgent need for him to make some reply. Mainly, he feared that, if he didn't handle this situation satisfactorily, he might be evicted from his lonely sanctuary. For reasons he couldn't articulate, it seemed preferable to remain isolated in his bedroom for as long as possible.

With superhuman effort, Jake managed to excavate the words "all right" from the depths of his brain and convert them to barely audible speech. He hoped that would be sufficient to appease her. Actually getting out of bed to take a shower was beyond the realm of possibility. She might as well have suggested he climb Mt. Everest this morning. He had been able to get to the bathroom a couple of times a day so, Jake reflected to himself, he still cared enough to avoid soiling the bed. So far anyway. But showering would require an inconceivable boost of energy. And, Jake mused, who cared if he stank? He wasn't going anywhere.

He didn't object in principle to getting up, but his body seemed to be composed of shapeless protoplasm. This protoplasm was composed of a gray, heavy matter. Oddly, the outside world seemed to consist of similar gray, dull matter. Apparently, some membrane separated Jake from the environment. Looking back, he couldn't say when this metamorphosis had occurred. Gradually, his body had lost any distinct structures while at the same time becoming too heavy to move. Compared to him, Jake concluded,

Kafka's Gregor Samsa had had it easy. True, Gregor's transformation had occurred overnight, which would be horribly shocking, whereas his had been so gradual as to be barely perceptible. Still, at least a grotesque insect can still move about and even enjoy itself. A shapeless, five hundred pound amoeba is a useless organism with no hope of a meaningful existence. To the human eye, Jake had maintained his usual form, which, Jake realized, only further complicated his situation as others found his newly acquired passivity to be inexplicable.

Gregor had managed to die. Jake wondered how. If nothing else, he should die of starvation soon enough. He hadn't eaten all day yesterday. (According to the bathroom scale he had already lost 27 pounds, but he no longer belonged to the reality of scales. In his new reality, based on how difficult it was to lift himself out of bed, he estimated 500 pounds might be more accurate.) Or perhaps sleep deprivation would do it. He had been sleeping in brief spells all night and day. He couldn't be sleeping much, though, as he felt more exhausted than when he'd run a marathon five years earlier. Every movement required herculean effort.

At times he could momentarily recall his former life. He'd been a good journalist until the layoff three months ago. Jake supposed his kids probably would have said he'd been a decent father. Inexplicably, his wife still seemed to consider him a human being.

Jake suspected it had all started with the layoff. He couldn't really pinpoint it, but that seemed as good a theory as any. After all, he had been on an upward trajectory, on a fast track to success, a locally well-known journalist. Then, instantaneously, he had become just another nobody. The scene played itself over and over in his mind: Jake's boss calling him into his office, discoursing somberly on the state of the economy while Jake, only half-listening, was still mulling over the piece he had been in the middle of writing. He conjured up an image of his boss concluding his economic treatise, and explaining how much he regretted having to let him go. On that occasion, his metamorphosis had occurred abruptly as he went from king to pauper. Jake had tried to find work at another newspaper, but the economy had collapsed for everyone. He had accepted the idea of finding any paying job, but had failed even at that. After a while he had felt like the world was passing him by.

Jake now judged himself to be a worthless creature. Venturing into the world offered nothing but more opportunities for failure. He preferred to seek solace in his room, away from the unjust world, shielded from further disappointments. He spent his time wallowing in self-pity and melancholy. He let the tears flow. First he had read in bed. When that had overwhelmed his powers of concentration, he had switched to watching TV. Gradually, he had stopped showering or shaving. He stayed in his underwear in bed. Leah had thought she could jar him into action by refusing to sleep in their bed until he cleaned up. But by then he didn't care anymore. Even the tears had dried up.

Now it seemed like he'd been overcome by a physical adversary of some sort. The adversary had become Jake and he felt as though he had, in fact, become an oversized amoeba with no body, no mind, and no free will— all of which had gradually faded away. He had a vague idea of how he could move as an amoeba, by shifting his pseudopod off the bed and letting the protoplasm flow into it. But he was no ordinary amoeba and was weighed down by a toxic heaviness. His protoplasm didn't flow. It had turned into a murky, semi-solid substance that stuck to his membrane and induced a paralyzed yet chaotic state within him. Being only a metaphorical amoeba just made matters worse as he was still expected to fulfill his human role.

Jake's two sons, though, seemed to be gaining awareness of their need to adjust to life without a functional father. At first, David, who had turned ten last month had tried to check on him in his room every couple of hours. A month ago, Jake had still been capable of sitting in the living room during David's birthday party. He hadn't spoken with any of David's friends, and after a half hour, he had begged off, claiming to have a migraine. He hadn't thought the other kids noticed too much, though Leah told him later that David had been in tears when he realized his father wouldn't be there as he blew out the candles. When he'd come in to thank Jake for the model rocket Leah had given him as their present, his father's lack of enthusiasm about launching it with him had caused the tears to well up again. Jake's younger son, Josh, had barged into the room numerous times at first, bringing games to play or just hopping in bed with him. He'd gradually given up on Jake as he'd realized he would always find an excuse not to play. When Josh had asked if he didn't like him anymore, Jake had discovered that he too could still shed a few tears. Josh barely entered the room now and almost seemed somewhat frightened of his father. Perhaps, Jake speculated, he was the only one who perceived that Jake had become an amoeba of sorts. Leah had informed him that Josh had started acting out in his second grade class so it was obvious that he hadn't been unscathed by Jake's transformation. Both Josh and David were getting poor grades for the first time and their teachers had contacted Leah to convey their concerns. Jake felt remorseful that he was in some way to blame, but he saw no solution other than extracting himself, like a rotting tooth, from their world. Being brutally honest with himself, he acknowledged that, sometimes, he barely cared. And for not caring about his children, he felt he surely deserved to die.

Despite his apathetic state of virtual nonexistence, stabbing pangs of guilt afflicted Jake when he thought of Leah. She couldn't hide her red eyes or the dried trail of tears on her cheeks. He knew she was trying to pull him back into her world, but he just continued his descent into a barren nether world, leaving her behind to suffer. Lately, she had threatened to get him help whether he wanted it or not. He didn't want to hurt her, but he figured, in the end, she'd be better off without him.

It seemed to Jake that years had passed since his wife's admonishment to take a shower. He hadn't yet made it to the bathroom. He heard steps coming towards the room. These were not Leah's footsteps. Someone knocked and opened the door before he was even close to issuing a reply.

"Good afternoon, Mr. Burnham. I'm Jim Curtis. I'm a mental health clinician from the mobile crisis service. How are you doing today?" Jim introduced two other members of his crisis team who stood quietly behind him.

Jake heard Leah's stifled sobs from the hallway. He was too taken aback to reply. Besides, his thoughts were flowing at the rate of molasses in the remnants of his brain and he would have needed at least fifteen minutes to compose a coherent response.

"Looks like you're having a rough time with this depression. That can be treated, you know. We think you need some help getting out of this funk."

Leah peeked into the room. "I'm sorry Jake. You need help. I'm afraid you'll die in there!"

Jim asked Jake to come with him to the hospital for a more thorough assessment. Jake had no will to resist. Nor could he move. But somehow, Jim guided him to a sitting position and got him to stand up. Jim seemed to have experience with amoebas like him, Jake noted. Jim reassured him repeatedly that depression could be treated. He thought Jake could get started on an antidepressant and set up an appointment with a therapist once he made it to the ER. Jake felt some sense of relief on being delivered into someone else's hands, although Jim's words sounded far too rosy to him.

As they emerged from his home into the gray world, Jake noticed there wasn't a single cloud in the sky.

Follow-up

Dr. Katz first met Jake Burnham on the psychiatric inpatient unit. By the time he had arrived at the emergency room, where he met with the psychiatry resident on call, a sense of hope had already begun to seep into his amoebic protoplasm as he described it. He agreed to a voluntary admission, which was a relief to Leah, who had been anxious that Jake would refuse to leave home with the mobile crisis team clinician and would end up being involuntarily committed to inpatient care. She feared this would have been an unpleasant process.

Once on the unit, Dr. Katz interviewed Jake and quickly concurred with the admission diagnosis of a major depressive episode. In his admission note, he commented that Jake's severe and persistent depressed mood, lack of motivation and loss of interest in all activities were cardinal symptoms of depression. The diagnosis was also supported by his multiple other symptoms including insomnia, low energy level, weight loss, difficulty concentrating, slow movements, minimal ability to produce any speech and feelings of worthlessness.

Despite Jake's thoughts that death would bring relief, Dr. Katz did not feel that the risk was particularly high as his suicidal thoughts appeared to be passive in nature i.e. Jake lacked any real intent or plan to immediately end his life. Jake was admitted to an unlocked unit.

Given the severity of Jake's depression, Dr. Katz considered the option of ECT- electroconvulsive therapy. He explained to Jake that ECT, while much maligned by public opinion, remains the most effective treatment of severe depression. However, both Jake and Dr. Katz preferred to start with medication in combination with both individual and group therapy.

Dr. Katz started an antidepressant of the SSRI (selective serotonin reuptake inhibitor) class and titrated the dosage up quite quickly, hoping to spur Jake on toward a speedy recovery. Jake's slowness of movement verged, at times, on complete motor immobility. On a few occasions, he was observed holding his arms up in the air for at least five minutes and staring blankly at the wall. Dr. Katz suspected an element of catatonia, which sometimes accompanies severe depression and thus also added lorazepam, a benzodiazepine in the valium family, hoping to alleviate these catatonic symptoms. He realized that catatonia would be another indication for ECT treatment, but this remained "plan B".

Jake's mood began to improve significantly during his second week in the hospital. Given the severity of his initial presentation, Dr. Katz was surprised by the swift response and even worried that the antidepressant treatment might have unmasked an underlying bipolar disorder, but fortunately no manic symptoms emerged. Jake became much more verbal and was able to benefit from individual counseling. He also developed an initial action plan regarding freelance work he could pursue as a journalist. He looked forward to using his free time to commence work on the memoir he had long dreamed of writing.

By the end of his third week on the inpatient psychiatry unit,

Jake was doing well enough to be ready for discharge. Follow-up was arranged with an outpatient therapist and Dr. Katz continued to see him for medication management in his outpatient practice.

A couple of months later, Jake's freelance work was well underway, although his income fell far short of previous levels. Most importantly, his wife and sons were immensely relieved and delighted that he had returned to the human world. They were wary, initially, that he might slip back, but with time, they felt more confident that life in the Burnham home was back on track.

A Song for Kevin

Sometimes the obvious is revealed to us as a life-altering revelation that shifts the tectonic plates of our world. Such was the case when Kevin sat in a stuffy, cramped bedroom listening to Taylor Swift singing "Love Story" on the radio. Suddenly he realized this was not just another famous singer. Taylor was signaling directly to him that she was the girl he had played with in his hometown while growing up in New Hampshire. Her website claims she grew up in Pennsylvania, but he knew that was simply a ruse to lead astray the busybodies. It was a lucid, penetrating spiritual connection that grabbed him by the shoulders and shook him out of his reverie. He wondered how it had taken him so long to comprehend her message. But now she was in his face, almost screaming out her love for him. He hadn't rested his head on a pillow for two nights, but energy jolted his body into action.

He couldn't wait to tell Jim and Gary, his neighbors, who tormented him and taunted him for being the man he was. "We'll see who's 'psycho' now," he muttered to himself. He relished the thought that they'd finally have to admit he's the superior being in their apartment complex. He's the historical figure living incognito, using lowlife scum like Jim and Gary as camouflage. Taylor had tracked him down though. It amazed him that her love for him had been burning so strongly, so invincibly all these years. How had he been so oblivious? Reading between the lines of her song's lyrics, he instantly deduced that she had hopes of settling down with him. He must be the one she sings about...the one she first met when they were both young...the one who would be her prince.

That evening he encountered Jim and Gary in the entranceway as he returned from throwing out the garbage.

"Wassup looney boy?" shouted Gary with his usual knack for the humiliating epithet.

"I'll tell you what's up, imbecile," he replied with as much cool composure as he could muster. "Ever heard of Taylor Swift?"

"Yeah, why?"

"She and I are about to become an item."

Jim and Gary broke into guffaws of ridicule. Jim launched a verbal assault: "Do you really believe this shit, man? I mean are you bullshittin' us or are you stupid or just plain nuts?"

Kevin explained to them that the lonely 12- year-old girl in torn jeans and tattered sandals who once invited him to venture out of their neighborhood for a picnic lunch had grown up to become a famous singer. She and her family had disappeared from town only a few weeks after that picnic on the bank of the Saco River. He had forgotten about her until she sang "Love Story" for him that day. He was still reeling from the impact.

"Hey, I don't have time for this crap. You're lucky we're good Samaritans—otherwise you'd be in a straitjacket by now," sneered Jim.

"Was that girl's name really Taylor Swift?" Gary mockingly inquired.

"These people always take stage names, idiot," Kevin parried. "Back then she went by the name of Linda. I don't think I knew her last name. But she's clued me in through her songs. It turns out the reason she writes her songs is to communicate with me."

"Dream on, psycho boy," snarled Jim as he turned to Gary and proceeded to ignore Kevin.

Kevin decided the truth would out eventually. Every dog has its day, he consoled himself, and his day was coming down the track. Blithely, he spun away from these two, dismissing them as local nobodies and sauntered through the entrance to what now struck him as a rather gloomy, dilapidated apartment building. Visions of an imposing hilltop mansion flitted through his mind as ecstatic warmth suffused his body.

The immediate dilemma was how best to respond to Taylor, letting her know he had received her message and eagerly awaited their too-long-delayed reunion. Would he convey his feelings and dreams best in a letter or would a face-to-face meeting be preferable?

The solution presented itself in the most spectacular and unforeseen manner. Emanating from the radiator, Taylor's voice greeted him and professed her lifelong love for him. At first he searched for her in the apartment. For a fleeting moment he wondered if Jim and Gary had contrived some sort of practical joke. He soon ruled out any such chicanery.

In no uncertain terms, he shouted out his response to Taylor: "Your love will be requited! You will forevermore be the sole purpose of my existence! I am happy to live for you and will do anything to make you happy!"

To his shock, Taylor's voice proceeded to describe her erotic fantasies about them in graphic detail. He felt the heat rise to his face as he blushed in embarrassment. There was not even an iota of doubt in his mind; they were destined to be together and their union would brook no further postponement. Taylor herself insisted he must pack his bag and get on a train. He asked her for her address. She advised him to come to her next concert. A quick internet search turned up her scheduled events. The next concert was in five days at Club Nokia in Los Angeles. He had no credit card so he couldn't purchase the online tickets, but he'd get in, he reassured himself "come hell or high water" as his father used to say. L.A. was a long way from New Hampshire, but there could be no insurmountable obstacle for their relationship. In fact, he would head off that very evening.

Stuffing some clothes and other essentials into his duffel bag, while focused on the glorious future that awaited him in his promised land, he was soon prepared for the journey. He lit off for the state highway and stuck his thumb out. Several cars passed him by, irritating him beyond expression. Enraged, he kicked a boulder beside him. To his great relief, headlights appeared like eyes of a sympathetic alien seeking him out, slowing down as they drew nearer.

The driver lowered the passenger window: "Hey, Kevin, where ya' headed?" asked Mr. Landon, owner of Landon's Pharmacy. Kevin explained that he needed to get to the bus station in Concord. "Okay, hop in," he replied. "I haven't seen you in ages," Mr. Landon commented.

"No, I haven't been taking the lithium for a month now, and I'm doing better off that stuff."

"So, where are you taking a bus to?" he inquired.

Suddenly he felt an overpowering urge to blurt out everything that had transpired. His speech couldn't quite keep up with his thoughts, but that didn't deter him from trying.

"I was listening to the radio—the one I got at Walmart, like my uncle worked at for a while, I'm never working in that place, maybe I'll go back to college, be a professional then we'll be a fine couple because she told me over the radio to come get her we'll get married have kids she loves me unbelievable how direct she was about sex like a text like in Texas or somewhere where they do that maybe an English flat right on their backs, I'm going to California to marry Taylor Swift..." It was a lot to explain, but, somehow, he got the major point across because Mr. Landon seemed to get his drift.

"Okay, Kevin, you sound pretty excited, but just slow down a minute okay? I've got to make a stop first at the New Hampshire State Hospital pharmacy before the bus station." The mere mention of that place usually gave Kevin the creeps, but tonight he was in seventh heaven no matter what happened. This would give him more time to chatter on, carefree and naturally high on love.

Eventually, they pulled into the hospital entranceway. Mr. Landon instructed him to sit tight in the car. It was all he could do to keep himself from busting loose and just dashing off to California by foot.

A few minutes later, two burly security guards approached him. They seemed friendly yet intimidating, the kind of people, he realized, you don't want to aggravate.

"Hello sir," one of them greeted him. "We'd like you to come inside to talk to someone for a minute."

"I don't have time now, man—I'm about to catch a bus to see my fiancée in California."

"This won't take long, buddy," the guard reassured him, as he firmly grabbed hold of his arm. For a wild instant, Kevin considered just taking off, but somehow that didn't seem like a wise move, so he allowed the guard to lead him into the hospital.

The guards directed him toward the admissions office. This whole situation was starting to seem bizarre to him. How had he ended up in a psychiatric hospital, even if he was just waiting for Mr. Landon? Suddenly, intense frustration fed the fire of his irritability. How would he explain this delay to Taylor? He no longer trusted these guards or anyone around him. He feared they were trying to keep him from Taylor. He screamed for Mr. Landon to hurry up, but, instead, it seemed he had summoned another two security guards. The next thing he knew they were grabbing all his limbs. He couldn't believe it.

"What the fuck are you doing?" He felt he was totally losing it. He wondered if he sounded like a Jim or a Gary as he shouted: "Get your redneck hands off of me! Do you know who I am? I'm on my way to see Taylor Swift. Call her up and ask her yourselves!"

Within minutes they had his arms and legs bound to a bed. A psychiatrist entered the room, asking him tons of questions, but he couldn't even respond to most of them; he could no longer focus on anything except Taylor. Why was this happening?! These people were all trying to stymie him, to keep him stuck, not just in his hometown, but in a psych ward. He wondered if Jim and Gary had conspired with those guards to ruin his life. He could tell the doctor didn't believe him. He thought he was being labeled "crazy" and the doctor was speaking euphemistically when he called it a "manic episode". He told Kevin he was too out of control to leave. They were keeping him there! Taylor's voice boomed out from nowhere: "Run Kevin, come to me!"

He tried to do what she asked of him. He did everything in his power, but didn't have a chance against those beefy, macho guards. Everyone had betrayed him—Jim and Gary, Mr. Landon, the security guards. He thrashed, he hollered, but he accomplished nothing other than incensing himself even more.

***

He has been at the hospital five weeks now. He has learned not to mention anything about Taylor or their mansion on the hill. He takes their pills; he keeps his passions under wraps. He maintains his composure; he's pleasant toward everyone. This way, he figures, he'll soon "earn" that weekend pass and be on his way.

He tries not to let them shatter his nascent dreams. But Taylor hasn't spoken to him in a few weeks. He can't imagine that she could be tired of waiting for him or that she'd ever allow him to step foot again in that sea of despair--in that desolate, ramshackle apartment building where two bullies would greet him: "Welcome home psycho boy." She's probably just giving him some privacy.

Isn't she?

Follow-up

These days, Dr. Katz considers Kevin to be a success story in his outpatient practice at a community mental health center. He has several close friends, a decent job and he hasn't required hospitalization in over three years. It hadn't always been this way. The admission to New Hampshire State Hospital had been the first of a series of similarly heartbreaking inpatient stays for Kevin.

Each of those involuntary hospitalizations had been preceded by Kevin's decision to stop his lithium for bipolar (manic-depressive) disorder while he was mired in depression. He knew this was one way to pull himself out of his desperate lows. The problem was his mood would then swing too far in the other direction. Each time he ended up in a manic state of euphoria with the same grandiose delusion that Taylor Swift was in love with him. He heard her professing her desire for him. He had boundless amounts of energy despite almost complete lack of sleep. His thoughts raced through his mind and he talked a mile a minute. It was difficult for others to keep up with his thoughts as he flew from topic to topic ("flight of ideas" in psychiatric jargon). He became more impulsive, making irrational plans and often running up a debt as a result. It took weeks in a hospital to stabilize his mood, but each time the manic mood and accompanying psychotic symptoms (voices and delusions) did resolve eventually, usually with lithium alone, but on some occasions an antipsychotic medication was added temporarily.

Dr. Katz felt powerless and frustrated as he spent an untold number of outpatient sessions striving to persuade Kevin that stopping his lithium, might vanquish his depression, but would only lead to more suffering in the long run. Kevin agreed with this conclusion as long as his mood remained stable. Once he became depressed, though, this line of reasoning was quietly rejected. The allure of a life of marital bliss with a famous singer, albeit fueled by a delusion, was irresistible. His manic episodes would come on so abruptly that Dr. Katz usually only realized he was no longer taking the medication as prescribed when he showed up in an emergency room due to seemingly bizarre behavior. Dr. Katz had tried using a variety of antidepressants, but these all triggered off manic episodes for Kevin so, instead, he had hoped to optimize the lithium dosage. He wished he had better treatment options for bipolar depression. The lithium alone was, unfortunately, far less potent at preventing his depression than his mania.

When lamotrigine, a newer mood stabilizer that sometimes seemed to be especially effective in treating bipolar depressive episodes became available, he added it to Kevin's lithium. This seemed to help, but Dr. Katz attributed his progress mainly to the intensive case management and other therapeutic supports at the community mental health center. He considered the clinicians in these programs true heroes, working on the front lines of community mental health. They spend their days in the field on the patient's turf, helping to solve practical problems in the real world with the goal of recovery in the sense of finding genuine life satisfaction. The case managers, or community support workers as they preferred to be called, delivered medications to Kevin in his apartment and ensured that he did not miss any doses. They also persuaded him to join in group activities, including a book group and art group in which he gradually established lasting friendships. The employment counselor supported him in obtaining training in computer skills, writing up a resume and applying to jobs, and ensuring he had enough support to succeed when he started working at the local library. It was all these supports and the consequent changes in his life that seemed to finally convince Kevin that living in the real world, despite all its travails, was far more satisfying than the delusion of a future paradise. Once that realization occurred, Kevin no longer had to be convinced to take his medication. Nor did he believe that medication had been the entire solution. He felt empowered by all the steps he had taken to forge a better life for himself and was determined to keep building his future on solid ground.

Just in Case

"Three times one is three, three times two is six, three times three is nine. There we go- three multiples of three."

The symmetry, the reassuring repetition of this mantra-like arithmetic calculation serves as a balm to Bob Walsh's troubled mind, albeit a most ephemeral one.

Finding such relief is a full-time occupation, a never-ending quest for fleeting salvations. It's not just selfish comfort Bob seeks; he strives to protect all those whom he loves. He employs many distinct yet interlinked methods to accomplish this goal.

Omnipresent, malicious germs must be battled with superhuman perseverance in Bob's world. To do so entails washing and rinsing his hands 33 times after touching a doorknob, shaking hands or handling money. Bob believes that one's existence is so precarious. But for years he had helped his parents, sisters and brother survive by checking innumerable times that the stove burners were off and the doors were locked at night. Ensuring safety is no easy feat. These days he lives alone, but, still, on those rather infrequent occasions when he does venture out of the home, Bob has to return three times to verify the stove burners are off.

Bob reminds himself he shouldn't complain though. Whatever he does now is child's play compared to the task he set himself when he actually was a child. He wasn't ten years old yet when, seated in the backseat of his father's car, his daydreaming was interrupted by the sight of a public building with a trefoil nuclear fallout shelter sign. After his father briefly explained the meaning of this sign, Bob began to ponder the potential impact of nuclear war. It terrified him to consider that not just his family, but the entire planet would be wiped out. He couldn't stop dwelling on this possibility. It kept him up at night. Eventually, he took action. Bob developed rituals to save the world. He arranged his socks by color; he buttoned his shirt up from the bottom while skipping over the third highest button, saving this for last after buttoning the top two; he opened and closed his door three times before entering his room (but was socially savvy enough to do so only if no one was watching). He made up an elaborate prayer and uttered it three times to himself as soon as he returned home from school. He fervently hoped the President was doing all in his power to prevent nuclear war as it seemed far too much responsibility to be shouldered solo by a soon-to-be ten year old. Why this recurrent "three" theme? Truthfully, he had no idea, but it seemed to preserve the world so he stuck with it.

As Bob got a bit older, he realized how ludicrous this all was.

"Mere superstition," he chastised himself. Yet far worse than superstition, for who spends half their day engrossed in combating their superstitions?

"What a colossal waste of time. This makes no more sense than avoiding black cats. And yet…what if there is a God and what if this is the way God wants me to worship Him? What if I really have prevented catastrophe and tragedy by my rituals? Okay, so it's one chance in a million, but one is not zero."

So just in case, he continued his soothing rituals, and, to his dismay, even added new ones.

Even so, he managed to live an almost normal existence for a while. He attended college. He got a decent job. He married a good woman. Granted, she was greatly irritated by his need to spend over an hour in the shower after sex, but she never guessed the real reason and was quite supportive when he finally "confessed" his need to wash off any offending germs. She was less accommodating when their daughter was born and he was next to useless when it came to changing diapers. Bob tried dutifully to help out, but his hands would shake from the panic and after a few weeks of intensive washing they were more chapped and raw than ever before. Nor did she appreciate it when he started getting up at least five times each night to check that their daughter was still breathing. Each time he got up to ensure his daughter's well-being Bob knew he was actually destroying the very edifice of his life and love, brick by brick. Yet he felt like a helpless observer, rather than the self-destructive protagonist of this tragedy. The final straw for her came after he lost his job. He could never get to work on time due to all the rituals. She left him soon after he was fired. Those were dark days indeed. He raged against the compulsions and obsessions.

"How could I let such nonsense ruin my life?" he often reproached himself.

He went a couple of days without counting, without washing his hands more than a few times a day. But soon, uncertainty and insidious anxiety ensnared him in their cruel grasp once again.

Not long afterwards, a new source of worry reared its ugly head in Bob's mind when he started his job search. He was living in New York City and using the subway to get to his job interviews. As he waited on the platform, he noticed how close some people were standing to the edge. How easy to push them onto the subway tracks.

"What if I did it? How much control do I have over my own mind?"

Not much, he feared. He envisioned himself impulsively

rushing over and shoving the young man in front of him to his death. What an atrocious thought.

"Could I really be that evil? Three times one is three…"

Sweat trickled down Bob's face. His heart thumped against his rib cage. He was so shaky that he had to lean against a column. He looked quite a fright, and even though it was a NYC subway station, a middle-aged woman approached him. Bob's first irrational thought was that she had somehow detected his murderous inclinations. Then he realized he must have turned pale as a ghost as she kindly inquired how he was feeling and if she should call an ambulance. He recovered enough to brush her off and reassure her it was just a "touch of the flu".

Bob was horrified by these constant, monstrous thoughts and his job search ground to a halt. Whenever he approached a subway stop, he was hounded by the obsessive thought of shoving an innocent would-be straphanger off the platform. Although he knew he would never really do such a thing, he suffered from this "doubting disease" and "knowing" something was never quite sufficient to allay fear. He imagined the victim's plaintive screams followed by police officers tackling him. As these repugnant thoughts became vivid, terror-inducing images in his mind, Bob realized he had to flee the city. He could not live with the fear of turning into a murderer, even if the chances of acting on such an abhorrent impulse were infinitesimally small.

Bob Walsh relocated to the woods of Maine following his divorce. When he first arrived to his country home, a neighbor, from a few hundred yards down the road, came by with apple pie to welcome Bob to the area. He recognized the moment as a chance to start over. The woman was beautiful but shy. He sensed that she feared being humiliated by having her kindness rebuffed. And yet, he did not invite her in. As soon as the thought entered his mind, he rebelled against this intrusion which might ultimately bring with it a need for more rituals of decontamination. He thanked her tersely and closed the door.

It's certainly not unheard of to be based at a remote site in his field of computer programming and soon he found work, although his salary plunged from its former levels. Explaining his recurring absences from conferences was a hassle but not an insurmountable one. He became more and more of a hermit. It was less exhausting to stay home alone. Lonely and depressing but less exhausting. Visitors only brought with them risks of contamination as far as he was concerned. Despite this isolation, he grew still more cautious and wore latex gloves when touching light switches, the keyboard and the phone in his own home. He sealed some rooms off to make them off limits completely.

Bob has come to accept the theory that the wiring in his brain is defective. He once came across the term- "reverberating circuit" in reference to unstoppable obsessions. It seems apt to him. They take on a life of their own and cannot be switched off.

Bob feels that his life is constrained by his own irrationality and actions, which seem ridiculous to him even when he is engaged in them. He has lost the love of his life. He barely sees his daughter. No friends cross his threshold. He could have been a leader in his field. Instead, he just barely ekes out a living.

He has tried to cure this strange ailment. The SSRI

antidepressants helped a bit, but his lifestyle didn't really improve all that much and he worried it might irreversibly alter vital neurotransmitters in some unforeseen, adverse manner. He never really gave behavioral therapy a chance; it seemed too overwhelming, not to mention profoundly embarrassing.

The existentialists speak of the absurdity of life. Bob has never grasped what was absurd for Camus or Sartre, but his existence seems to be the essence of absurdity. Most of his time is spent on senseless and meaningless activity. Why does he go on? He suspects that, in addition to the wiring errors, he is also hardwired to carry on. Is there something noble in doing so? He doubts it. He'd rather abandon all these demons of fear. He'd rather reclaim his life, engage in the world and seek comfort in the company of others. He does fully intend to start this new chapter of his life shortly.

But for now, just in case, he'll wash his hands.

Follow-up

This unfortunate soul did not actually start the new chapter of his life until several years later. Faced with the prospect of ever-increasing, self-imposed exile from the world, he finally overcame the force of procrastination and set up an appointment with Dr. Katz.

Dr. Katz wasn't surprised by his long delay in seeking treatment, but, nevertheless, it saddened him when he considered how long Bob Walsh had allowed his suffering to go unchecked, and, in fact, proliferate. Like many others who struggle with severe obsessive-compulsive disorder, Mr. Walsh's embarrassment regarding his behaviors and thoughts, which he recognized as irrational, had prevented him from divulging them even to a professional for far too long.

Dr. Katz also wasn't surprised that his illness had only partially responded to past treatment with SSRI- selective serotonin reuptake inhibitor- antidepressants. He had taken these medications at relatively low doses and for relatively short periods of time. More importantly, he had not received cognitive behavioral therapy, which Dr. Katz considered to be at least as essential as medication in treating this stubborn illness.

After discussing the diagnosis and treatment, Mr. Walsh accepted a prescription to start a new SSRI antidepressant trial with a goal of titrating the dose upward to optimize the response. He also set up an appointment with an excellent cognitive behavioral therapist in the community. Dr. Katz was pleased to have access to a well-trained, experienced cognitive behavioral therapist as he knew full well that such therapists were too scarce in many locales.

With his therapist, Mr. Walsh undertook the arduous, but ultimately rewarding, task of changing his thinking patterns as well as his behaviors. He learned to recognize his cognitive distortions such as magical thinking, black and white thinking, overestimation of risk and his disturbing tendency to fuse mere thoughts with actions in his mind. With his therapist's guidance, he developed a plan to gradually extinguish his compulsive behaviors by exposure and response prevention. He postponed washing his hands and limited the number of hand washings when fearing contamination. Initially, he could only touch his phone or door knob with his fingernail, but he steadily, albeit slowly, progressed to the point he could even carry his garbage can with his bare hands.

In a belated gesture of gratitude, Mr. Walsh invited his erstwhile welcoming neighbor over for an afternoon coffee break. That was the day he grasped that treatment had already changed his life. He opened up to her about his struggle with OCD. Empathy came easily for her as she struggled with her own anxiety and the relationship blossomed over time.

Mr. Walsh never completely rid himself of annoying compulsions, but his victories were sufficient to allow him to end his hermit-like existence. He reached a point that his illness no longer could force him to sacrifice his dreams.

Messages from an Ex and/or Current Girlfriend

Friday 1:05 pm:

Hi, lovey, it's me, Heather, you probably weren't expecting a voice mail from me so soon, but I miss you already. We're going to be apart for a week—that seems like eternity. I don't know if I can take it. When I saw you driving away, I felt like I was clinging to the edge of a precipice. I need you to hold me and keep me from being sucked into a black hole. I really should have hidden myself in your suitcase like I joked about! I really do want you to enjoy your trip and conference though. You deserve a week off from me. I know I'm a handful sometimes. Call me as soon as you can. Kisses and more!

Friday 5:11 pm:

Keith, haven't you arrived there yet? I got your text at least, but I really need to hear your voice. You know what I think of texts. They're just too cold and impersonal, there's no real meat to them. Call me! I know it hasn't been too long and I tried not to bug you so soon after my last message, but...I miss you. I'm lonely...call!

Friday 8:15 pm

It was sooo great to talk to you. You know you're everything to me. You're my whole world and everything seemed all right again after you called. But that was a few hours ago. It seems like forever. If you get a chance, could you call me again tonight?

Friday 9:02 pm

Keith, guess who? Your lonely heartbroken girlfriend...Call!

Friday 10:17 pm

Thank God you finally called. I was beginning to feel kinda low on your list of priorities…Anyway, good night, Call me in the morning.

Friday 11:03 pm

Hi Keith, it's Heather; I just want to say one last good night to you. It'll be a quick call, don't worry. I'll wait up for your call…

Saturday 12:45 am

Oh, put your ring tone on mute did ya? Way to ignore me, smartass. Or are you in bed with some slut already, you heartless bastard! Gone a few hours and already hooked up with someone else. You cruel prick! Well, you're messing me up big time. Hope you're happy. I hadn't binged like that in over a year- 3 packages of oreos and then I barfed 'em all up. See what you're doing to me, you fucker?

Saturday 2:30 am

Oh Keith, Keith, please forgive me. I'm so, so sorry about that message I left you. You know I didn't really mean it. You're the light of my life. I just felt so alone and desperate and then after I binged, I just hated myself. It actually got worse. I don't want to worry you, but I cut myself. It was just the butter knife, just enough to be my pressure relief valve so I wouldn't explode. But I'm fine now. I just wish I could delete that last message. Love ya.

Saturday 8:24 am

I'm so honored you found the time to call me this morning—such an important, busy guy like you. A regular fuckin' national treasure. You think you're God's gift to women, don't ya'? I could tell you were forcing yourself to sound like you cared. I don't know why I ever believed you'd be any different from all my other asshole boyfriends. Okay, so you don't actually knock me unconscious like Joe or hold a loaded gun to my head like my last loser boyfriend, but you're just as mean in your own way. I should

44

have just sworn off men forever after my uncle did what he did to me in the barn all those years. Or don't you believe what I told you? Even my mother didn't believe me. She just screamed at me for supposedly being a "provocative worthless slut". She even threatened to kick me out of the house if I caused any more problems for the family. Trust nobody. But no, naïve me, I keep trying again and again. I'm sitting here with a bottle of vodka. Who knows what I'll do by the time I've gulped this down? You'd better call ASAP!

Saturday 2:03 pm

Sorry, so truly sorry. No you don't need to cancel your conference and come home. I'll be fine. I don't know what came over me. All of a sudden, I felt like my whole world had come crashing down. Everything and everyone was against me. My whole world turned dark and gloomy. I can't even remember why I felt that way. I must have passed out from the vodka. I just woke up and heard your message. Thank you so much for checking on me and calling.

I'm so lucky to have a saint like you. How did a bitch like me pull that off?! I can't wait till you get home. I'll make it up to you. Get ready for the most exciting sex of your life, big boy!

Saturday 7:35pm

Okay asshole, do I have to spell everything out for you? Of course, you should have come home. I slashed my wrists and almost drank myself to oblivion. What does it take for you to think of someone else for a change? Things are out of control here. And where are you? Off screwing around with some "colleague" probably. You think just because you called every hour, I should be grateful or something? Sorry to inconvenience you, you selfish dork. Don't bother calling. You won't have to trouble yourself with me anymore. This so-called relationship is over. We're history. Go to hell!

Sunday 9:31 am

Keith you have to forgive me, please, please forgive me! I went too far this time. I felt like you'd abandoned me here all alone. I wanted to crawl up in a ball and die, I should have. Instead I went to Jessica's house. She wasn't there, but her husband was. I spilled out my heart. I couldn't help it. But wouldn't you know it; he was just pretending to comfort me so he could get in my pants. Keith, he just got me while I was vulnerable. I feel so sick. I can't stand myself! I'm trying not to cut again. I feel like a human nuclear reactor. If you don't want a meltdown, pour some coolant in my core. Call me. I need you more than ever! Of course I don't really want to break up with you. I don't know how those crazy words ever came out of my mouth last night. If you ever leave me, I'll end it all, I swear!

Sunday 5:22 pm

Oh, I feel so fantastically great now. I think that's just what we needed to boost our relationship to a whole different level. Do you realize we talked for over 3 hours? I bet a few years from now we'll look back on this…on my mistake last night as just a bump in the road to our personal paradise.

Monday 8:30 pm

Keith, you've got to help me. I'm at the Emergency Room. I don't know what possessed me. I was feeling so good this morning. Then when I didn't hear from you, I thought maybe you were having second thoughts about us and then I thought who could blame you? I hate myself for sleeping with Jessica's husband. Why wouldn't you hate me too? I just felt so hopeless. I didn't really want to die; I think I just wanted some peace, just to escape all this crap for a few hours. I took out the bottle of Benadryl and just stared at it for a while. I tried to call you, but just got your voice mail again. I OD'd on the whole bottle. I realized I'd screwed up and called Jessica right away. She called an ambulance. Now the doctors here might not let me go home unless I'm with someone. The crisis counselor told me I might be "borderline personality"— whatever the hell that means. He said it means I'm too impulsive and have mood swings and can't control my anger. Basically, he said everything about me is unstable and that I create chaos in the world around me. I hate to admit it, but I guess that does sound a little like me. I agreed to start therapy and to go to a group to learn "coping skills" and how not to fly into rages all the time and how to accept myself, but also change myself so I can handle stress better instead of OD'ing and things like that. I wrote it down…it's called dialectical behavior therapy. I want to give it a try. I know I can do it, but they still don't want me to go home alone. Please, please call. I'm sorry to ruin your conference, but I really need you here now. There's no way I could be alone now; the doctors are right. I love you Keith.

Monday 9:25 pm

Oh Keith, you came through for me; I knew you would! You're the most amazingly wonderful man in the world. The doctor even said you sound like a nice guy. You're probably driving now so you don't have to call back. I just wanted to let you know I'll be all ready to go as soon as you get to the ER. The doctor just has to sign something. This doctor's kind of cute. I think he was flirting with me—the way he looked in my eyes. Anyway, thank you so, so much. I really just called now because I wanted to hear your voice on your voice mail message. Keith, I think I was just scared or something. I feel like I've somehow grown from these few roller coaster days. I'll never do that stuff—cutting and OD'ing again. I feel more mature, more sure of who I am and what I want. I want you! Can't wait to see you! If you do get a chance…you know, maybe stop at a rest area on the way…and call me!

Follow-up

By the time the date of her therapy intake arrived a few days later, Heather had lost interest in attending dialectical behavioral therapy. She convinced herself everything would be fine now that Keith had returned home. Keith and Heather made a valiant effort to save their relationship, but Heather's mood swings and intense emotions proved too much for Keith to bear. Her fury seemed to be triggered by the most insignificant comments or sometimes by a lack of response. She threatened to cut her wrists so frequently that Keith stopped taking it seriously, but, occasionally, she did in fact cut herself. At the emergency room, the doctors became less sympathetic and even rebuked her for coming in with only superficial cuts, when other patients were there with urgent problems.

Heather could not tolerate being alone and quickly found a

new boyfriend after Keith called it quits. She continued the pattern of tumultuous relationships for several more years. Sensing it held some key to escaping her suffering, she had kept the recording of her voice mail messages that Keith had once given her in an effort to explain why he couldn't handle her emotional intensity. From time to time, she would replay the recording and would be filled with self-loathing. Usually, that was followed by a burst of resentment toward Keith. But one day, she reacted differently, and called the outpatient mental health clinic for an appointment.

Once again, she heard a therapist explain that her impulsivity and the lack of stability in her moods, behaviors and relationships were actually quite common in people with borderline personality disorder. This time she followed through with the recommendation for dialectal behavioral therapy. In the group, she met others with similar struggles, which eased her loneliness and misery. Together, they learned and practiced new ways to interact with partners, friends and the world.

She also met with a psychiatrist, Dr. Katz, who gradually tapered her off five of her six medications. He realized that she had encountered doctors along the way, who had sought to ease her distress by medicating it away. Unfortunately, medications were of very limited benefit for her personality disorder. Hope had been provided in the form of a pill, but had fallen short each time. Now that she was learning healthier ways to cope, she was eager to rid herself of these useless crutches. She had experienced several episodes of significant depression and chose to remain on one antidepressant, but agreed to discontinue the second antidepressant, the antipsychotic medication, the two benzodiazepines and the sleeping medication that had been added to her medication list over the years.

Eventually, she felt ready to take a break from therapy. Her antidepressant would be prescribed by her primary care doctor. Dr. Katz marveled at the progress she had made. Her relationship was steady, which was a new experience for her. She was well-liked at her job and had made lasting friendships there. It had been a treacherous path, one bordered by precipices. More struggles were sure to come, but she had emerged into a far more stable and secure world.

Lumpy Shoulders

Dr. Gorman looked like a man on a mission, as usual, as he barreled past the ER beds, heading directly towards his intern, Dr. Katz. Dr. Katz, had a fleeting thought of conducting a study of the correlation of interns' pulse rates with their proximity to Dr. Gorman. He had no doubt what the results would be in his own case after his first week of work in the emergency room. Dr. Gorman had no time for fools, but clearly felt himself surrounded by them. With his towering stature, long, scraggly beard and wild-eyed stare, he resembled an angry biblical prophet more than an ER attending.

"Katz, go see the young woman in bed 3. I checked on her quickly. It's an easy case. Get her out of here ASAP. We've got a congestive heart failure headed in and I might need your assistance."

Before Dr. Katz could ask for any details about "bed 3," Dr. Gorman had seemingly teleported himself to the other end of the ER to check on a stroke victim. But he had said it would be an easy case so, Dr. Katz hoped he could handle it without having to submit himself to Dr. Gorman's ridicule, which was the fate of any intern who, stumped by a case, dared to seek his guidance.

Lisa's chart was disappointingly uninformative, but Dr. Katz was relieved to see this would indeed be a nice change from the medical train wrecks he'd seen so far in the ER. She was only twenty and unlike most patients he had seen that shift, she didn't seem to have the combination of uncontrolled diabetes, hypertension, heart disease and emphysema treated with at least a dozen medications, all on top of the latest, acute problem. This was indeed going to be quick and easy.

As he pulled aside the curtain and introduced himself to Lisa, he was struck by how out-of-place she seemed in the ER that evening. Here was a young, healthy-looking, fairly attractive woman in the midst of a sea of pain and suffering. She looked even angrier than Dr. Gorman, but her timid posture was a marked contrast to her obvious rage. She sat slouched on her bed as though trying to curl herself into a compact ball so as to attract no attention. He asked her what was bothering her.

Like a cornered cat she pounced on him: "Oh great, they assigned me the clueless medical student!"

"No, I'm actually a first year resident as I mentioned, and I'll be reviewing everything with a senior physician," he lamely reassured her. Reluctantly, she provided monosyllabic responses to his questions as he attempted to obtain her medical history. He marveled at her ability to convey sarcasm so effectively with a single word.

"Well, if you're not clueless, why do you even have to ask why I'm here? Isn't it obvious?" Dr. Katz detected a slight softening of tone in her verbal assault.

His bewildered countenance must have evoked some pity as she continued on without awaiting his response. "It's my shoulders; I can't take it anymore. They're grotesque! I'm sorry for being nasty, but I've been to three primary care doctors about this and they were just plain rude and unhelpful to put it mildly."

Sensing an opportunity to keep the clinical interview brief, Dr. Katz suggested they proceed with the physical examination. She seemed pleased that she wasn't going to be bombarded with more questions.

Lisa was patient with the exam and had a look of anticipation, clearly hoping he'd provide some straightforward but revelatory answers. Yet, he had detected nothing remarkable on the physical exam. He started to perspire, thinking he must have missed something obvious if it was causing her this much distress.

"Could you point to the exact area of your shoulder that's a problem?" he requested, hoping this would provide him with the clue he needed.

"Are you blind too?" she groaned. "I have lumpy shoulders. It's not an exact area, it covers both shoulders—this disgusting pad of fat. It's been getting bigger and bigger over the past few years. I know what you're thinking now, but this is an emergency. Let me tell you, if I don't get help with this, I'm not sure I can go on living!" Noticing his look of alarm, she reassured Dr. Katz that she didn't mean she'd kill herself that night.

He took a step back and scrutinized her shoulders. "Well, I really don't think it's that bad, but maybe there's a little bit of fatty deposit," he mumbled, having half-convinced himself that, with his rapidly developing, astute clinical observation skills, he could indeed perceive some slight deviation from normal shoulder anatomy.

With a sudden flash of insight, he knew he had cracked the case. He recalled that Cushing's syndrome, a result of excess cortisol production, could cause a "buffalo hump." He thought that was supposed to be a fatty hump on the back of the neck and between the shoulders, but this must be a variant. He quickly asked her about symptoms of Cushing's and continued the physical exam, checking for any of the signs he could recall, but came up empty-handed. Nonetheless, he figured he must be on the right track. Dr. Gorman would be impressed with him for once. He even recalled a few tests needed to confirm the diagnosis. Dr. Katz informed Lisa that he had some ideas, but would first like to run them by his attending.

Upon his approach, Dr. Gorman, grunted, "It's about time. It's a good thing I didn't need you to do any real work here. Are we ready to send her off?"

"Not yet, it's turning out to be more complicated than it seemed at first. She has a slight buffalo hump possibly. Should we order a 24-hour urinary cortisol test and dexamethasone suppression test? Should we also go ahead and get an MRI of her pituitary and adrenals?" No sooner had he suggested this slew of tests, than he realized he had committed a cardinal sin in Dr. Gorman's eyes- mindless ordering of tests. But his situation was even worse than that.

Glowering at him, Dr. Gorman demanded, with world-weary exasperation, "Are you serious? I assume you've never seen a buffalo, let alone a buffalo hump, but the only test you need to order now is your own vision exam. This is a case of GMG-gornisht mit gornisht. Do you know what that is?"

Dr. Katz had to admit he didn't know that either.

"Jesus, I'm filled with apprehension to think what else I'll discover that you don't know. GMG is 'nothing with nothing'. Don't you know any Yiddish?"

"Other than 'schmuck', not really," he replied, hoping Dr. Gorman wouldn't realize how passive-aggressive that remark was. Dr. Katz was beginning to wonder if he might be in the running for an entry in the *Guinness World Records* book for number of blunders committed by an intern in a single shift.

"So you don't know Yiddish or buffalos. There's absolutely nothing wrong with her shoulders. And that's not the location of a buffalo hump anyway, not even an invisible one. Now send her home. You can refer her to a counselor if you want."

"Still, Dr. Gorman, I feel a bit uncomfortable just sending her home. It seems like there's got to be something going on if it's causing her this much distress. It's making her incredibly discouraged, and she might also have a clinical depression even though she denied most of the symptoms of depression."

"Okay, go look up body dysmorphic disorder, offer her an SSRI antidepressant and stop wasting everyone's time."

"Dr. Gorman is an asshole, but he's a bright asshole", Dr. Katz told himself, so he knew he should go check the *DSM*—the psychiatric diagnostic manual—for a quick review of body dysmorphic disorder. Before returning to Lisa, he did manage to find a tattered copy of the *DSM* and learned that body dysmorphic disorder consisted of pathological, excessive preoccupation with a slight or imagined physical deformity. This could actually result in severe impairment of functioning.

"That bastard Gorman is right again," he acknowledged.

Sheepishly, he dragged himself over to Lisa. "Lisa, the good news is there doesn't seem to be any serious medical problem or any need for tests." He went on to explain the diagnosis and suggest the possibility of referrals for counseling and antidepressant medication.

"Okay, enough, stop your condescending bullshit. 'Body

dysmorphic disorder' is just your fancy jargon for 'it's all in your head.' Just because you doctors are too stupid to see what's in front of your eyes, you condemn me to a life of misery. How will talking to a counselor fix these monstrous shoulders? 'No serious medical problem,' you say! Let me tell you what 'nothing serious' has done to my life. I haven't been on a date ever, not even once. I don't want to set myself up to get hurt when the guy realizes I'm some kind of ogre- the Hunchback of Notre Dame. I haven't been to the beach since ninth grade. Even that time, I had to pretend I was keeping my shirt on because I was sunburned even though I would have loved to have cooled off in the water. There's no way I'm going to put on a freak show in a bikini. I don't go anywhere. I don't even have friends anymore. I'm taking a few on-line courses, but that's about it. I can't be seen in public. I wear baggy, frumpy clothes so people won't notice my lumpy shoulders so much, but it's no use. What kind of life is this?" She burst into tears of utter despair.

Dr. Katz tried to explain that he understood she was suffering, but he hadn't found a medical disease affecting her shoulders. He told her he wasn't saying she had "nothing" and that body dysmorphic disorder was a real illness. He again recommended counseling and seeing a psychiatrist as whatever this problem was, she must agree it was making her depressed. "I really don't notice anything wrong with your shoulders," he added, rather unhelpfully.

"Has anybody ever even commented on your shoulders?" he asked.

"Well, people aren't rude enough to be truthful. But, yes, this all started when I went to summer camp when I was 14. We'd played a game of flag football and one of my teammates said I was a good football player. There was something about her tone that got me thinking about what she meant. Later, months later, I eventually realized, she probably meant I didn't need to wear shoulder pads because I've got natural ones."

Dr. Katz could barely follow her line of reasoning. "Don't you think you read way too much into some innocent comment made by a teenage kid six years ago? It sounds like a simple compliment to me."

"You're just trying to be nice. You even said before that you see 'fatty deposits.' Listen, if I could just get the lumps off my shoulders, my life would be great. I could have friends again, go to college, meet a guy, and just be normal again. Please, tell me how I could get these lumps surgically removed."

Her desperate entreaty left him momentarily dumbstruck. It shook his confidence in his medical world view. Maybe plastic surgery was worth a try if it'd transform her entire life. He knew it would be futile though and only leave her in greater despair when she discovered there was no surgery for psychological lumps.

"All I'm asking is that you tell me whom I should contact to discuss this. Please don't block me from my only chance for happiness. I just want to have a life."

Against his better judgment, he relented and explained that, if such surgery were done, it would be performed by a plastic surgeon. She managed to extract a specific name from him. He warned her: "No honest surgeon will do this operation, though, because there really isn't any indication."

"So give me the name of a dishonest surgeon," Lisa cried, a wisp of a smile shining through her tears for the first time. "I'm kidding. Thank you for listening and giving me the plastic surgeon's name. You're a good doctor. You actually care."

Dr. Katz wasn't so sure. Was it wrong to provide her some sense of hope and relief, even if it was only evanescent? Of course it was, he concluded. Dr. Gorman would skin him alive if he found out he'd even mentioned the option of surgery. She'd most likely lose all hope when the surgeon declined to operate. Or, if the surgeon foolishly agreed, she'd sue him when her living hell and nonexistent lumps persisted after surgery.

Dr. Katz let her know the surgeon would probably want a psychiatric assessment so she might as well set up an appointment. To his surprise, she agreed to this as well as counseling. He wondered if she was just feeding him what he wanted to hear, but she seemed genuine when she smiled again and added, "I know I need a back-up plan in case it turns out that all of you are right and it really is in my head."

"Well, maybe that would be a relief in a way," he suggested, hoping to encourage her.

Lisa shrugged her "lumpless" shoulders, and Dr. Katz headed off to let Dr. Gorman know he was ready for his next patient.

Follow-up

Feeling guilty about the referral to the plastic surgeon, Dr. Katz had phoned the surgeon the next day to explain his predicament and apologize for the inappropriate referral. The surgeon had reassured him that he would meet with Lisa anyway and encourage her to focus on psychological treatment.

Many years later, Dr. Katz was pleasantly surprised to receive follow up regarding Lisa's condition by way of a letter sent to his psychiatric clinic:

Dear Dr. Katz,

You probably don't remember me, but, in case you do, I thought you might appreciate hearing how things turned out after I met you in the emergency room over ten years ago, demanding you help me with my lumpy shoulders.

I went to see the plastic surgeon you recommended, but you were right, he declined to operate. He told me surgery wouldn't solve my problem and would probably leave me even more depressed. He agreed with your suggestion that I see a psychiatrist and counselor.

I've wanted to thank you for listening to my story. I think that's what made all the difference. You were the first person to really listen to what I had to say without brushing it aside or belittling my suffering. Even though I didn't convince you of the revolting ugliness of my shoulders, I knew you realized something was terribly wrong.

So, I did set up that appointment with the psychiatrist. He was the third person to label my problem "body dysmorphic disorder." He also thought I was depressed. He started me on good old Prozac and explained it could help with my depression as well as my obsessive thoughts about my shoulders. He also referred me to a cognitive behavioral therapist who had worked with people with "my problem." I thought he meant people with lumpy shoulders, but he really meant people obsessed with body flaws that no one else noticed.

My therapist got me to identify all kinds of irrational, automatic thoughts. It took years for me to accept a more nuanced view of my appearance. Even before that, we came up with a plan for me to gradually get out in public despite my concerns about my shoulders, and eventually I started hanging out with friends. My therapist wouldn't let me avoid the world anymore. And I had to stop checking my shoulders in the mirror a million times a day. At first I felt awfully uncomfortable around people, but I think the mindfulness skills helped me just tolerate those bad feelings and wait for them to pass. I was able to stop the Prozac and rely more on these new coping skills.

Don't get me wrong. I sure don't think I'm any beauty queen. But I've been able to push myself to get a life. I'm married now and my husband, like everyone else, says he sees nothing wrong with my shoulders. I'm pretty sure that other people really don't see it and maybe there isn't anything to see. In any case, I've stopped letting it control my life.

So thank you for taking the time to listen to me. You probably didn't realize how much that helped.

Respectfully yours,

Lisa

P.S. Please accept my belated apology for calling you a clueless medical student.

What If?

"Mom, is it in two weeks that we're going to New York City?" Tonya Camdens's 11-year-old daughter's eyes radiated excitement. She knew her daughter, Beth, had been anticipating this trip for months now. She had never been to the Big Apple, but seemed convinced this must be the most thrilling locale on the planet. Beth had high expectations of the museums based on what she had read in *From the Mixed-Up Files of Mrs. Basil E. Frankweiler* and had seen in *Night at the Museum*. Ms. Camden had been hoping the excitement would be contagious.

Since her teenage years, she had kept a painstakingly detailed journal, attaching great importance to accurate recall of even minor events. In this personal journal, she not only recorded significant conversations with her daughter, but also acknowledged her internal dialogue with brutal honesty.

"Yes, Beth, exactly two weeks from today."

That's assuming we don't get the flu or get injured between now and then. What if we do, though? I wonder how difficult it would be to cancel the flights and hotels without losing too much money. The Broadway tickets would be a total loss for sure. I'd go ahead and cancel this trip anyway, but Beth is so excited.

"How long is the flight? It'll be fun seeing the city from the sky!"

"It's just a little over an hour."

I hope there's no bad turbulence. My therapist hit it on the nail when she diagnosed me with 'What If? Disorder'. On the day we fly, I should probably use the clonazepam my doctor gave me to relax when my "generalized anxiety disorder" (his term for my neurosis) gets out of control, but what if it makes me too drowsy and I don't wake up when we land? Or what if it makes me act bizarrely or slur my speech like a drunken bum? I'll already be exhausted from not sleeping the night before. My stress levels maintain my state of insomnia and fatigue all the time, so I can assume it'll be a sleepless night before the trip with everything I've got to worry about. Plus, I'll be too anxious that my alarm won't go off and we'll miss the early morning flight. Might as well just stay up all night. It might be nice not to feel so tense for a while though, so maybe I should take that medication. Besides, I don't want to have a panic attack on the plane.

"Mom, will we see *Lion King* the day we get there?"

"That's the plan Beth. Hopefully, things will go according to plan."

"Well, why wouldn't they, mom? Don't be such a worry wart all the time!"

"Good idea."

Why, wouldn't they, hmmm…? Well, for starters, our flight might be canceled or delayed if the weather is bad. What if the flight is overbooked? Not to mention, planes do crash sometimes. Okay, they say it's the safest form of travel, but it's all relative. Speaking of flights, I need to make sure to do the early check-in. What if the hotel messed up our reservations and we're stuck in

Manhattan with no place to stay? I hope I remember to pack everything we need. I'm getting another headache just thinking about all the potential catastrophes. Beth is right though, I need to get a grip on my worrying. I know she puts on a brave front because she thinks I'll freak out even more if she mentions her worries. All this worrying is what drove her father away; I don't want to lose her too. Or worse, turn her into a 'worry wart' like me. Her teacher already commented that she seems a bit anxious…

"I want to try my roller blades in Central Park!"

"Okay, don't forget to pack them."

One more thing to worry about—a roller blading injury. I hope the bicyclists watch out for little girls on roller blades who don't stay in the lane. I suppose even that'd be better than getting mugged in the park. What if we need to find medical care there? Will our insurance give us problems with out-of-state services? What if I'm the one who gets hurt? What would Beth do? What if she gets lost in the city or even kidnapped? What if she falls through an open manhole? Okay, now I'm probably getting a bit ridiculous.

"Mom, how many steps are there in the Empire State Building?"

"I don't know Beth, but we can ask them when we're there."

I'm guessing there are enough steps to give me a heart attack if I have to use them. What if the elevator breaks down when we're at the top? No, wait, even worse, what if it breaks down while we're on it? I'm breaking out in a sweat already. Can those cables snap? I'll have to figure out a way to get out of going to the top without disappointing Beth too much.

"Will we get to see the Statue of Liberty?"

"We'll have to see if there's time. There won't be time to do everything on one visit, unfortunately."

Just surviving this damn trip would be satisfactory. Let's hope al-Qaeda doesn't choose to strike again while we're there. What if they use a nuclear weapon this time or spray us with anthrax?

"Mom, I can't wait to ride on a subway!"

"Yes, that's the best way to get around."

Assuming no one pushes you onto the tracks, that is. And that's another likely place to get mugged.

"I hope our hotel is right near all the action!"

"I think it is in a pretty convenient location."

What if the bedbugs think it's a convenient location too? And what if we're stuck in that hotel because of pouring rain the whole time? On the last day, we'll need to leave our suitcases in the luggage storage room in the hotel after check-out because our flight isn't until evening. I always worry someone will steal them from there…

"I'm going to lie down for a bit, Beth. I'm a bit tired and I think that'll help with my headache."

"I wish we could just 'fast forward' to two weeks from now!"

"Two weeks will be over before you know it."

I'll be in my grave before you know it too, for that matter. What if I could experience pure pleasure…have fun uncontaminated by worries…wholeheartedly enjoy one little trip?

What if…? What if…?

Follow-up

Tonya survived her trip to New York, but bemoaned the extent to which her worrying had suffocated genuine enjoyment. She was determined to quell her anxiety enough to fully share the joys her daughter experienced.

Tonya had been in therapy for years and she knew that her excessive worrying and anxiety, her clenched jaw, muscle tightness and constant sense of being on guard for impending disasters were consistent with the diagnosis of generalized anxiety disorder. She had also experienced a number of full-blown panic attacks and her anxiety had led to periods of outright depression.

This time she was determined to implement and build upon the insights she gained from therapy. Her anger at her situation served as a critical impetus for change.

Dr. Katz explained that antidepressants are also used to treat anxiety disorders and worked with her to find an antidepressant that she found helpful. She began intensive psychotherapy, initially meeting twice per week with her therapist. She felt relief talking about her situation and anxiety. She came to recognize that many of her worries were triggered by an underlying fear of mortality-hers and her loved ones. She also grew very adept at identifying and correcting her distorted ways of thinking that amplified her anxiety such as overgeneralizing, jumping to (negative) conclusions and catastrophizing over minor setbacks. She learned to meditate and focus on the moment rather than on 'what ifs'.

Tonya never achieved the goal of tranquility to which she aspired, but she no longer felt controlled and stalked by anxiety. She felt gratitude for the many moments of pure happiness that life offered.

The Final Escape

The first time it appeared, shortly after his twenty-first birthday, the terror of confronting the unknown immediately seized Evan. Lying in bed, feeling vaguely uneasy, he suddenly perceived the silhouette in the periphery of his bedroom. It wasn't that it threatened him directly, in those first moments, or seemed all that concerned with him, but its presence somehow disturbed what was left of life's equilibrium. He wasn't surprised by its fuzzy, impressionistic physique. He detested wearing his glasses and his poor vision often converted people into vague apparitions. But this one was different. Perhaps, its surreptitious movements or its aura of evil triggered his instinctive reaction of fear. In any case, he lay frozen in place, staring at this inscrutable creature, and sensing mortal danger. Then, it spoke—and its threatening nature was suddenly explicit. There was nothing fuzzy about its voice. Booming, precise, verbal grenades were hurled his way. "You are the devil's brother," it shouted in strident tones, over and over. Eventually-and probably it was no more than ten minutes later-it faded away from his bedroom. He had been too shocked to cry out that first time.

After that initial encounter, it had steadily and relentlessly insinuated itself into his life. Evan had grown determined not to scream as he had quickly learned that that would bring his parents running to his aid, and end with all silently admitting to themselves, with heartbreaking regret, that there was no aid to be given. Their priest had recommended they take him to a psychiatrist, but they were not believers in that sort of thing.

Instead, his parents had concluded that Evan might be susceptible to harsh interpretations of religion and urged him not to go overboard with this.

Then on one life-changing night, it had crept slowly closer to his bed. It shouted the usual insults and curses, calling him "devil's brother" and "sinner" and "pervert". It hissed that it would rape him and stab him. That night, for the first time ever, the demon didn't back away when Evan prayed. It shouted more loudly and reached out its slimy, octopus-like fingers and caressed his forehead. The ice-cold touch startled Evan. The gentle, cold caresses were incongruent with its pronouncements that he must die and burn in Hell for his sins. It proceeded to smash Evan over and over on the chest with shovels and swing axes at him. He jumped out of the bed, seeking shelter underneath it. He could contain himself no longer. From under the bed, he pleaded, "Save me!"

His parents had indeed come running. His father asked, plaintively, "What the hell happened, Evan? Why are you under the bed?" His mother noticed the bruises and through a veil of tears, wailed, "Oh my God, Evan, what have you done?" She begged him not to punch himself. This left Evan bewildered. What were they talking about? What made them think he had done this to himself? The cunning demon was nowhere to be seen.

On that occasion, his parents had finally overcome their distrust of doctors and had brought Evan to the local emergency room. From there he had been shipped to a psychiatric hospital. The doctors and nurses had been kind to him, but they seemed perplexed. Once he overheard snippets of the medical student's and resident's conversation as they discussed his case at the nursing station: "prominent visual hallucinations...somewhat atypical of schizophrenia... But he does have auditory hallucinations as well...seems a little too dramatic...could be malingering?...for what purpose? ... he's not working—maybe he's hoping to get disability...maybe that's why he's not responding to the medication...Well, if you reject the diagnosis of schizophrenia for anyone who doesn't respond to our antipsychotics, that'd be one way to reduce the prevalence of the disorder...he's not so atypical, no one really fits the DSM diagnostic criteria exactly..." He felt hurt that they didn't quite believe him or know what to make of him. They explained that they had chosen a good, but old, (cheaper) antipsychotic because of his limited insurance coverage. He took the haloperidol, dubious, yet maintaining a sliver of hope that it would rewire his brain and he'd realize the others were right when they said the demons were just products of his psychosis. He became stiff as a zombie, so then the doctors added a "side effect pill"—something called benztropine. This helped a bit with the stiffness, but added its own side effects, including constipation and cotton mouth. They eventually decided he was well enough to return home.

After his release from the hospital, the demon soon resumed its visits. Evan was desperate to describe his experiences with this creature, but he had vowed to himself never again to frighten his parents or to end up in a psychiatric hospital. He could not again bear to see his parents' looks of helpless terror. He did long to confide in someone other than them or his outpatient psychiatrist, Dr. Katz. In high school, there had been a couple of boys he considered friends, but they'd gone on to college while Evan lingered on in his parents' home, working at various menial jobs for a while, then gradually drifting away from the world. He had once hoped to find romance. While working at the supermarket, stocking shelves, he had met Stephanie who worked as a cashier. They used to eat lunch at the picnic table behind the store. Somehow, he felt at ease with her. They mostly just talked about their favorite music. Then one day, she nonchalantly dropped a bombshell. She'd be going away for a week on a camping trip with her boyfriend. Evan had suddenly realized how naïve he had been to think their superficial conversations meant she might be attracted to him. After that day, he ate lunch alone.

****

So there had been no friend to confide in; instead Evan had tried to bury this painful shock to his system in the clutter of his unconscious. Even now, at age thirty, though he almost accepted his life as a loner, he would have appreciated having someone who recognized the heroic nature of his struggles with his omnipresent demon. He didn't want to be told his brain was playing tricks on him again. Perhaps, though, it was better not to burden another with his tribulations. Evan had the feeling that it had even become too much for his psychiatrist to bear. Dr. Katz had run out of new antipsychotic medications to try and nothing had changed. Evan was intrigued by their exotic-sounding names and kept a list of all the medications he was given. He did have better insurance now so he had tried olanzapine and risperidone and aripiprazole and quetiapine and many other medications to boost their effects. For a while he'd even agreed to try clozapine, with its mandatory weekly blood tests, for what Dr. Katz termed his "remarkably treatment-refractory illness". The demon was still there. Only hope had vanished.

Some days, Evan thought his life wasn't really all that bad. He had no friends or girlfriend, but he still enjoyed listening to his heavy metal music. His parents tolerated his idiosyncrasies and left him alone for the most part. He didn't have the stress of work to deal with. The demon still harassed him, but it hadn't assaulted him in quite a few years. An elaborate prayer he chanted frantically to himself seemed to keep the demon at bay. He had developed a capacity to keep his torment to himself and thus avoid hurting his parents or returning to the hospital. And yet, he couldn't shake the constant, insidious, expectation of violation that so rattled his nerves. Although it hadn't acted on its threats, the demon had continued to constantly threaten to rape him and then rip his chest open.

It was shortly after his thirty-first birthday that his parents casually suggested he tag along on a shopping trip to Montreal- a day trip from their home. It might do him good to get out of the house for a change. At the department store in the mall, wandering down the long aisles, he felt shocked at the surfeit of objects to buy. It overwhelmed him to think of choosing from all these things. But no matter, he was just tagging along. Glancing towards the end of the aisle, he suddenly halted in his tracks. The demon was waiting there, pointing at him, whispering, "The devil's brother must die". He quickly about-faced, and strode briskly toward his parents, trying to conceal his panic.

"Mom, Dad... can we leave now!" They exchanged a puzzled look. His father reassured him that they were almost ready to head to the cashier. Evan stuck close by them, keeping his eyes closed and talking softly to himself to blot out the chilling threats coming from the other end of the aisle.

After an eternity, Evan, soaked in sweat, followed his parents out of the store where the walkway overlooked the courtyard several stories below. A wave of relief washed over him as they left the store. His parents tried to make small talk, but Evan was too distracted to participate. He strode single- mindedly ahead of them toward the elevator, hoping the demon could not match his speed.

Several seconds later, sensing a presence, he glanced over his shoulder and cringed in fright, as though shocked by an electric jolt. The malevolent, horrifying fingers of the demon were drifting toward his mother's head. Evan was torn between wanting to shout a warning to save his mother and not wanting his parents to worry that he was having a "panic attack" as they had referred to his display of terror at the time of his hospitalization long ago. He prayed furiously. But the demon turned to confront him, its shadowy face distorted by an unusually clear and omniscient, evil smile. The demon whispered, "Your time has come, devil's brother, you are mine now, your fate is sealed". It had never spoken with such finality, with such a sense of inevitable triumph.

It went on, telling him he had sinned beyond any hope of redemption. A tsunami of fear overwhelmed Evan. He managed only to utter, "Mom, Dad, run to the elevator now!"

His father responded, "Evan, everything's okay, you're just not used to getting out of the house. We'll stop for a bite to eat downstairs." His mother added, "Evan, try to enjoy the city; there's always so much energy in the air here."

Suddenly, the demon grabbed Evan's neck and emitted a piercing scream, "Die sinner, die!" Evan cried out in fright as he pushed the icy, arm away. The demon glared at him menacingly and slowly raised its hands, reaching out to grab him again. It kept up a constant barrage of denunciations and threats. Evan knew he had to act quickly. The cruel, murderous demon would turn its attention to his parents once it was finished with him. His parents were blind to this peril so only he could avert catastrophe.

Some chase after fool's gold; some sacrifice all for a painted whore; some follow a false Messiah. In Evan's case, the route to salvation came to him in a flash. Instinctively, he knew what had to be done to liberate all of them from the demon's clutches.

Sensing something amiss, his father stood before him and moaned plaintively, "What the hell's happening, Evan?" Evan shoved him aside, dashed to the railing overlooking the courtyard and flung himself over. His mother wailed, through a veil of tears, "Oh my God Evan, what have you done?" His father fell to his knees and pounded the floor with helpless fists as strangers far below rushed toward his son's inert body.

Too late to save Evan, who had finally escaped his demon.

Follow-up

Dr. Katz discovered Evan had completed suicide by reading of his 'unexpected death' in the local paper's obituaries. A wave of devastation swept over him. He had grown attached to Evan over the years. He had few patients with schizophrenia who had shown such complete lack of response to multiple treatment trials. In fact, he had often been amazed at how well many of his patients with schizophrenia fared. He believed in recovery, at least in the sense, that people could lead fruitful, satisfying lives without being controlled by their psychotic symptoms. Of course, some of his patients stopped taking their medications and relapsed, but Evan always took the medication faithfully. He hoped he had given Evan some comfort by meeting with him and offering a sympathetic ear, but he felt frustrated that his treatment efforts seemed so futile in ridding Evan of his demons. Nevertheless, Evan had maintained his integrity and pleasant demeanor. He never became bitter and even seemed to have accepted his lot in life.

Dr. Katz's shock on learning of Evan's suicide immediately led him to question himself. Could he have done something to prevent it? Had he missed a sign that Evan was in distress at their last visit? What could have been the final straw for Evan? Colleagues tried to offer support, but Dr. Katz was unconvinced by their reassurances that he had done all he could, wondering if these were spoken primarily out of kindness.

Dr. Katz knew Evan's parents had never had much confidence in his ability to help their son and now it seemed their skepticism had been justified. Nevertheless, he felt an obligation to reach out to them.

With some trepidation he called Evan's parents, expecting them to let loose with a fusillade of accusations. Evan's father answered the phone. To Dr. Katz's surprise, he seemed fairly calm and very pleased to hear from him. He reassured Dr. Katz that they would appreciate his presence at Evan's funeral.

He met with Evan's parents at his office a week after the sparsely attended funeral. They spoke of their sadness and self-doubts. Dr. Katz realized that Evan's parents had been asking themselves for years what more they could do to ease Evan's suffering. Though they all had more tears than answers, Dr. Katz felt it had done them good to share their pain. A bond of sorts formed between them, which seemed to Dr. Katz to be an appropriate memorial to Evan.

Seasonal Acrophobia

It was a bluebird day as skiers are wont to say, not a pesky cloud in the azure sky. With temperatures in the mid-twenties and a light breeze out of the southeast, nature was bestowing kindness and comfort that day. It was a fine day to start off the skiing season.

Bruce waited in the chairlift line with his eight-year-old son, David who was excited about their plan to try their luck on Devil's Playground, steeper and peppered with more moguls than any trail he had conquered last season. Bruce too, eagerly anticipated the thrill of racing down the mountain.

They shuffled along in the line, which was surprisingly short. As the parents and their two young daughters in front of them boarded the quad chairlift, Bruce and David were already gliding into place for the next chair. The line was short so no strangers would be riding up with them. Bruce knew the ride up would be harrowing due to his fear of heights, but he'd been through that before and the reward of a thrilling descent would more than compensate for that tribulation. At least, he hoped that's how it would work this winter.

As the chair scooped them up and passed by the first lift pole, Bruce felt confident. He reminded himself that thousands of adults and children have uneventful chairlift rides every day. With the safety bar down, there was really no way to fall out. Nevertheless, a sense of foreboding nagged at him. What if he had a panic attack leading to a heart attack and was stuck on the lift. The delay until getting medical help would be fatal. Another ridiculous preoccupation, he tried to reassure himself. Soon the crescendo of heart palpitations slammed into his chest as panic proclaimed victory over his tepid reasoning. Waves of heat radiated from Bruce's heart and dizziness raised the specter of fainting. Slipping through the bars and off the chairlift would of course inevitably follow, Bruce fretted. If only his feet were planted on solid ground, he'd be laughing at that preposterous thought. As they approached the mid-station, the potential option of getting off was enough to dissipate the sense of doom. Bruce was once again sure this would pass just as had all his previous chairlift rides.

The family ahead of them had their safety bar raised as they prepared to unload at the mid-station. Suddenly, the parents realized that one of their daughters, who looked to be no more than six years old, had remained on the lift. The mother screamed desperately: "Stop the lift!", but the lift kept moving. The attendant came out of the booth and explained vacuously that there was nothing to be done. The girl would have to continue on to the top where another attendant would help her off. Immediately following the mid-station, the lift went over a deep gully leaving the lift riders at least five stories high for a seeming eternity. Meanwhile, the girl was lying on her back on the chair. The safety bar was left in the raised position. She screamed for her life and writhed with fright. Horrified, Bruce yelled repeatedly to her to just sit back and not to move, and thankfully, she listened.

Somehow this represented a revelation of sorts for him. Not even a young, wiggling, panic-stricken child without a safety bar had fallen out of her seat. And despite the stress, he hadn't fainted or suffered a heart attack. He hadn't even considered his own plight as he was totally focused on reassuring the girl that she would be fine if she just sat back. This burst of confidence lasted him for the rest of the day, notwithstanding a few twinges of anxiety.

By the next weekend, Bruce was looking forward to experiencing his newfound bravery on the chairlift. An eerie sense of calm enveloped him as they stood on the lift loading line. He almost eagerly awaited the chair. Perhaps, the chairlift ride would become the interlude of boredom or a chance to relax that it seemed to be for other people. An opportunity to chat with one's fellow sojourners on the lift. Once seated, he tried to focus on the enjoyable aspects of a day of skiing with his son. They spoke about David's new ability to carve his skis around moguls without reverting to a snowplow.

As the chair passed over the mid-station ramp, however, Bruce's awareness shifted abruptly to their height above the slopes. Fear seized him with its cold, sharp talons. Several seconds later, the familiar crescendo of heart beats and waves of heat had returned with a vengeance. He was sweating, his heart was pounding and he sat paralyzed with fear. The lift continued on relentlessly. Nevertheless, he figured he had at least a 50/50 chance of surviving to the top and then losing himself in the delight of cruising down the mountain with his son.

Turning to his father, David asked: "Dad why is your face so red and sweaty?"

Bruce decided to explain a bit about his fear of heights, partly to distract himself from the physical sensations that were attacking him.

David's face lit up as he exclaimed: "Wow, so you're really brave to go on this lift even though you're so scared!"

As this sympathetic interpretation seeped through the shroud of panic, Bruce thought to himself, indeed, perhaps he was a sort of hero to persist in his Sisyphean endeavor while carrying his internalized burden, seemingly, in defiance of Death itself. He had repeated this impossible feat each winter. As the unloading ramp approached, the panic gradually subsided.

Eyeing the slopes as he glided down the ramp, he felt his lips part in a smile of gratitude.

Follow-up

Bruce had never considered his fear of heights to be problem warranting professional help. However, for a brief period of time he did see Dr. Katz due to unrelated panic attacks and this additional, longer standing problem came to light. Bruce still did not feel it was troublesome enough to justify traveling two hours to the nearest expert in cognitive behavioral therapy, the treatment of choice for specific phobias. Nor was there any local availability of the newer option of virtual reality exposure therapy, using a special head-mounted display to simulate the view from various precipices.

Instead, with some guidance from Dr. Katz, he developed a fear hierarchy of sorts, imagining a spectrum of anxiety-provoking situations from peering over a second story balcony to observing the valley below a rocky ledge in the nearby White Mountains. He ranked these on a 1-100 scale of "subjective units of distress" or SUDS and planned to gradually conquer his fear by actually visiting and habituating himself to each situation, beginning with the least scary scenario on his list. He had already learned a variety of relaxation techniques, including slow, deep breathing and muscle relaxation as well as reassuring thoughts, which he could employ while placing himself in the feared situations. Essentially, he decided to take Mark Twain's advice: "Do the thing you fear most and the death of fear is certain."

As Bruce preferred to handle this process on his own for the most part, Dr. Katz did not have a follow-up visit to assess his progress. However, one late February afternoon, Dr. Katz noticed a vehicle driving past him, skis mounted on the roof rack. Inside was Bruce who waved at Dr. Katz and smiled.

The Woman in the Attic

"So, you finally came down from the attic, you bastard!" Allen's wife screamed at him.

Once again, he tried to maintain his composure as he explained, "Sweetie, we live in an apartment building. We don't have an attic."

"Do you think I'm deaf and blind? I know what goes on up there. At least you could have the decency to admit it!" Alice glared at him with her dark brown eyes, squinting with outrage from under the partial cover of her bedraggled hair.

Alice's wheelchair seemed to swallow up her emaciated figure. She had lost weight while in the intensive care unit with pneumonia and now she barely touched her food so she continued to fade away. Allen had tried encouraging her to drink the Ensure supplements, but she accused him of wanting to poison her so he could go live with his mistress in the attic. Noticing the stains on her shirt, below her neck, her husband wondered if she might finally have started caring enough to eat, even if not caring enough to avoid spilling her food. But then he realized those were merely tracks left by the grease oozing from her hair.

The doctors had wondered if her medical condition had triggered off this radical change in personality. They even decided to check if she might have had a stroke. They came up empty-handed despite all their testing so they labeled it psychotic depression. She'd been a bit depressed ten years ago when she and Allen had filed for bankruptcy, but nothing like this. Back then, she'd seen a counselor and after a few months seemed to be back to herself. Now it seemed mounting frustration with her physical decline had led to invidious distortions of Allen's mundane comings and goings. She'd always been the more active one. Like a mutant brooding hen, her sitting seemed to be incubating some sort of growing rage.

Allen could barely recognize this woman who'd been his wife for forty years. It wasn't so much her malnourished appearance as her vicious countenances of hatred like a rabid wolf preparing to pounce. At first, after returning home from the hospital, she just seemed irritated by her ongoing, weakened state that prevented her from standing for more than a moment or two, let alone returning to her work as a school secretary. Despite his "sweetie" moniker, she'd always viewed the world with a bit of a sour attitude. Still, that was a long way from being a rabid wolf. She had started sitting for hours in her wheelchair, staring intensely at the wall or the door, as though expecting some sort of divine sign to appear there. Sleep eluded her, but instead of drowsiness, her insomnia induced a wired state of constant agitation and vigilance. Anxiety extinguished her habitual, mischievous smile. Immersed in dark thoughts, she barely responded to Allen.

Her doctor arranged a psychiatric consultation, following which she was prescribed Seroquel and Zoloft, an antipsychotic combined with an antidepressant, but, of course, she refused to be "poisoned" and never took a single dose. So she continued on this relentless, cruel descent into the depths of her personal hell.

Alice had always loved going for walks or jogging around the path at the local park. Over and over again, Allen entreated her to venture out of the home for a brief walk. As she grew weaker, he offered to push her around the neighborhood in her wheelchair, but she reacted with offense to the idea of receiving assistance. Her stubborn refusal to attempt a moment or two of enjoyment frustrated Allen immensely. Eventually, he resorted to taking walks on his own to escape the oppressive miasma of resentment that had permeated their apartment.

The situation went from bad to worse. One day, returning from his reprieve as he had come to think of his walks, Allen was greeted by a screaming banshee. Alice's rage infused her with adequate strength to hurl an empty vase at his head. He ducked just in time to avoid the projectile. "What the hell are you doing?" Allen shouted in turn.

"Don't play dumb with me! I heard you two plotting against me in the attic. I know what you're up to. You want to have me sent away so she can take my place here. I heard her laughing at me. She's just waiting to move down here. Well, I'm not going anywhere so screw you both!"

Tears streamed down Allen's face as he experienced a flash of empathy for Alice, who had good reason to be enraged given what she believed to be true. He knew explanations would be useless. He just stood there wishing he could have his loving wife back. Eventually, she calmed down enough to let him change the topic. Allen told her about the new cafe that was opening at the end of their street. She listened, while eyeing him suspiciously. Exhausted, he slipped away into the living room and flopped down onto the couch.

Collecting his thoughts, he realized this couldn't go on any longer. He had dodged the vase this time, but what might she do next time? It was as though a stranger, a monster, had taken over his wife's body. Her rage toward him was a seething volcano that might erupt at any moment, wreaking destruction. She was living in torture, which could be eliminated if she would only accept treatment. But she wouldn't. Her mind was no longer tethered to reality or rationality.

Allen crept quietly to the bedroom. He dialed 911, and struggled to control his tremulous voice as he let the dispatcher know his wife was psychotic and had tried to injure him and needed help urgently. After a few more questions, the dispatcher informed him the police were on their way.

Allen heard the doorbell ring. He sprang up and hustled to the door. Alice shrieked "don't you dare let her in our home! I'm warning you!" She removed a book from the bookshelf behind her and flung it at the door.

"It's not her," he replied. He opened the door, allowing two police officers inside.

"You sneaky bastard," Alice moaned. "You are going to send me away, aren't you? How could you be so cruel?"

Allen tried to explain to Alice that he felt she needed help while simultaneously whispering to the police officers that psychosis had ravaged his wife's mind, but he was overcome with sorrow, grief and incoherence. One officer, noticing his desperate state, uttered comforting words to him. The other tried to calm Alice down. He failed just as Allen had failed and soon had her in handcuffs as a last-ditch means to prevent her flailing arms from clobbering anyone as they rolled her away in her wheelchair.

Alice managed to look back over her shoulder, piercing Allen with intense laser beams of hatred emitted from her once-beautiful and gentle eyes.

Follow-up

Alice spent the first two days of her hospital stay glaring menacingly at the nurses and Dr. Katz whenever they approached her. The look of horror that seized hold of her face when Dr. Katz attempted to discuss the option of electroshock treatment or ECT for treatment of her psychotic depression convinced him that it would be unwise to broach the subject of any treatment for the time being.

Dr. Katz first had to establish a toehold of trust on the wall of suspicion she had erected around herself. Although her managed care insurance would apply pressure to implement treatment quickly or to discharge her, he had no intention of passing along this pressure to Alice. He spent time sitting with her and listening to her version of events. He did not broach the subject of treatment as he felt sure this would further alienate her. She refused to speak with anyone for the first few days of her inpatient stay, but over time she seemed to sense compassion for the sadness, desperation and fury that had engulfed her.

Allen called her daily, but was advised to postpone visiting until her rage toward him subsided. She did trust her roommate who persuaded her to participate in some of the unit's group sessions. She seemed to appreciate food again, although she only consumed a fraction of the meals served to her. By the fourth day her anger had softened to the point that Dr. Katz could discuss her diagnosis and treatment options. She remained convinced that her husband was having an affair with a woman in the attic, but she trusted Dr. Katz enough to try his suggestion that she take the antidepressant and antipsychotic combination previously recommended to her.

Dr. Katz was expecting an excruciatingly slow path to recovery given the severity of her depression and physical decline. He was thus pleasantly surprised by her remarkable progress after two weeks on medication. Alice even allowed Allen to visit and hug her. She was willing to consider the possibility that she might have been mistaken about the woman in the attic. She developed a more hearty appetite and began sleeping soundly.

By the time of her discharge several weeks later, she was able to laugh at the idea of this nonexistent woman in their nonexistent attic. Though still somewhat daunted by the goal of resuming her former life, she waved and smiled bravely at Dr. Katz as she left the unit, clasping Allen's hand in hers.

The Prisoner of War

Captain Phillip Reynolds observed with alarm that enemy troops were swarming the barracks. How the hell had the Japanese reached the Fort Bliss barracks of the 200th Coast Artillery in New Mexico? For a fleeting moment, Captain Reynolds tried to recall how he'd gotten back to Fort Bliss himself, but reprimanded himself for wasting time on reminiscing. His vantage point was far from ideal, but he sat frozen, hoping the enemy wouldn't detect him before he devised a plan for a counterattack. But no plan came to mind. In any case, he felt incapable of even standing up and he wondered if he'd been shot. The Japanese must have sent in their elite commandos for this mission as these soldiers were not moving in any formation, but appeared to be operating almost independently, with a calm, confident manner alien to ordinary troops in this bloody war. These troops weren't even Japanese.

They must be psychopathic mercenaries. The situation was as close to hopeless as any he'd ever seen.

"We're outnumbered! Get the hell out of the barracks!" Captain Reynolds shouted to his men. He'd be damned if he'd let the bastards capture him again. Summoning all his strength, he pushed himself to a standing position, despite what he could only assume must be grave injuries, and lunged for the door, thinking he'd regroup with his surviving troops outside, then figure out his plan for a counterattack.

"Phillip, sit back down! You'll get hurt!" Nurse Pamela scolded as she blocked his way from the exit.

"I'll have you court-martialed for insa... insabod... insubordination you traitor!" bellowed Captain Reynolds, shaking his fist at her, his face a writhing red mask of savage rage. Spit flew along with each word he hurled like projectiles at this enemy who sought to thwart him. If he hadn't been caught by surprise in his pajamas, she'd have treated him with the respect a captain deserved.

Pamela instructed the nursing assistant on the nursing home's special needs unit to page overhead for assistance in case Phillip got completely out of hand. She decided to give Phillip some space as she prepared a syringe of haloperidol for injection. Even with two hulking male aides standing by her side, Phillip continued to be combative, but eventually, they convinced him to retreat to his room and lie down. The aides held him still as Pamela administered the haloperidol. Phillip continued to curse as tears streamed down his wrinkled, mottled face until he finally succumbed to the deadening effects of the antipsychotic and sank into a tortured slumber punctuated by intermittent groans of despair.

Pamela wiped a tear from her eye as she wrote up her note back at the nurses' station. Mrs. Reynolds had told her about Phillip's experience in the Bataan Death March in WW II, or what she knew of it. He had never liked to speak much about it, but sometimes he'd awaken from a nightmare and describe what he had dreamed. It might be of his brother-in-arms, Ben, who had stumbled to the ground, exhausted and starving. Seconds later, a

Japanese soldier had bayoneted him. Phillip had described the look of searing anguish in Ben's eyes as he bled out as though pleading one last time to know what had become of the promising visions of his youth. Or he might have dreamed of his friend Henry's head rolling into a ditch, separated from his filthy, sweaty, emaciated body by a would-be, modern-day Samurai's sword. She knew that his anxiety whenever he got a stomach bug could be traced back to memories of other comrades succumbing to dysentery in the squalid prison camp. But for the most part, he'd managed to suppress such awful memories and go about his life. For some reason, Mrs. Reynolds told Pamela, the horrors of his prisoner of war experience had reemerged to drag him into the clutches of a terrifying past as he had descended into the murky swamp of dementia.

There had to be a more humane way of handling Phillip's "sundowning". Since his admission, a week ago, each day he had become agitated and disoriented by late afternoon, convinced he was about to become a prisoner of war again. She wondered if his evening incontinence was a consequence of fright. Although he couldn't dress or bathe himself, during the day he could appear quite composed and only revealed his substantial memory loss when asked specific questions. He had to search the depths of his memory for some words, but unlike most of the other residents, his impressive vocabulary had not yet evaporated or deteriorated into monosyllabic grunts. Even during the morning, though, he often seemed convinced he was in a barracks, but reluctantly tolerated his situation. But as evening approached, vexation and confusion overtook him. And every evening, she felt forced to play the role of a barbaric guard, as she orchestrated the ambush of Phillip and bayoneted him with the haloperidol syringe. She was determined to change the script tomorrow.

****

The next afternoon, Pamela herself escorted Phillip to the dining area on the unit to have his snack. His bewildered, edgy countenance softened momentarily to a wan smile of gratitude. She hoped he would view her as an ally rather than a sadistic Death March guard denying him food or water.

A half hour later, having briefed the unit aides, she announced cheerfully but calmly that it was time for a WWII victory parade. Pamela tried to maintain a veneer of confidence despite her trepidation that this scheme would end in a fiasco. She remarked to the residents in the dining area that she was delighted that WWII had ended. Only Phillip evinced a shred of interest in this comment.

Turning to Phillip, she implored: "Captain Reynolds, would you lead the victory parade?"

Phillip scowled and mumbled ,"What are you talking about".

"Yes, Captain Reynolds," Pamela acknowledged, "it's a last-minute celebration, but we really need your help."

Impelled by this appeal for leadership, Phillip stood up slowly but decisively, gradually straightening his meandering spine until his head was held high. Despite the food stains on his shirt and the spittle dribbling down his chin, Pamela marveled at how dignified he appeared. She could sense he was searching his balky memory for the appropriate command.

"Present arms," shouted Captain Reynolds, appearing relieved to have dredged up a command, although the hesitation in his voice conveyed his uncertainty regarding the proper order for this occasion.

Pamela and the aides set to work with the smooth precision of a troupe of dancers. Reassuringly, they helped the other residents to their feet, encouraging the more reluctant ones to join in. Those who resisted strongly were only urged to watch the parade. The aides brought over walkers and canes to those who needed them. Matter-of-factly, they kept repeating it was time for the WWII victory parade.

Pamela stood next to Phillip at the head of the parade. Glancing over her shoulder she felt overcome by compassion for her charges. Momentarily, the odor of urine and feces that permeated the unit had been replaced by an aroma of hope.

Then Mr. Adams, staring blankly down the hall, abruptly shoved his walker away, narrowly missing Mrs. Gomez who maintained her broad smile while wrapping her arm around Mrs.

Brown's waist in an ever-tightening embrace. The confusion caused Mrs. Margolis to intensify her perseverative demand to see her babies down the hall. Mr. Saxton resumed shouting his refrain of "Bitch, get away!" Mrs. Hendrix, the human equivalent of the Leaning Tower of Pisa, remained as perplexed as ever, but made a decision to sit back down, thus inadvertently instigating the others to do likewise. The commotion had distracted her from her constant moaning, but only transiently. Mr. Koslinski had shuffled off in the wrong direction. His pajama pants slipped halfway down his buttocks, revealing a soggy diaper. He launched into his usual plea, "Help me! Help me!" From out of nowhere, a disheveled and wild-eyed Mrs. Morgan materialized at Pamela's side to spit at her. "You idiot," she fumed at Pamela, echoing Pamela's own thought at that moment.

Chastened, Pamela realized she had to abandon her grandiose parade plan. But she was determined not to ruin it for Phillip. She quickly issued new instructions to the aides.

Fortunately, Captain Reynolds seemed unfazed as he observed the scraggly, ragged appearance of this motley crowd. He knew his troops had been through hell. They'd been starved, beaten, bayoneted, sickened, dehydrated, tortured and had surely suffered other abuses over the years. Of course, their uniforms weren't in impeccable shape. But he wasn't going to let that prevent the celebration. At least that was what Pamela imagined he might be thinking. She commented to him that the others were too tired to march, hoping to encourage this possible line of thinking.

"The war is over! We won!" she exclaimed. "Let's get this parade underway!"

Captain Reynolds with Pamela at his side and the two aides behind them trudged haltingly down the corridor. They were acknowledged by the usual cacophony of moaning and profanities along with blank stares. However, the nurse seated at the nursing station and a few surprised visitors clapped as they passed by.

All told, the parade lasted less than ten minutes, but it sufficed to burn away the fog of anxiety that constantly engulfed Phillip, revealing a glimmer of light. His evident feeling of well-being persisted longer than Pamela had expected allowing for an uneventful and relatively tranquil evening. Tranquil enough to avoid a haloperidol injection.

Phillip socialized with his comrades after the parade. Later on he went willingly to bed and the nursing notes indicated he slept soundly.

Pamela repeated the mini-parade every afternoon for the next four afternoons. She noticed relief wash over Phillip each time he received confirmation that the war was over.

By the fifth day, Phillip was clearly feeling more at home on the unit. He seemed to grasp that his fellow residents were not soldiers, though he still appreciated when Pamela reminded him that he was in a safe place now. He had fallen into a routine, sitting silently next to Mr. Adams at snack time, listening to Vivaldi on his CD player in his room after lunch and staring out the window at the verdant, beckoning woods out back. He even joined in some of the activities on the unit, like the current events trivia contest, albeit with an air of resignation. Pamela certainly wouldn't go so far as to describe him as content, but he had shed the desperate look of a trapped and defeated soul. Parades were no longer needed, but from time to time, Pamela cheerfully reminded him that peace had come and always addressed him as Captain Reynolds.

Follow-up

Dr. Katz had been consulted regarding the management of Mr. Reynolds's agitation and had hoped that this would resolve once he adjusted to the unit. It had been a rough transition, however, as Mr. Reynolds had delivered some well-placed punches to the frontline staff of the nursing home including two aides and a nurse. Thus he had reluctantly agreed to order the haloperidol injection if needed for severe agitation in order to prevent injuries to staff members on the special needs dementia unit. It was not unusual for new residents with dementia to exhibit aggressive behaviors when initially placed in the nursing home. Dr. Katz felt a bit depressed just walking into the nursing home so he could easily empathize with those newly placed residents who belligerently resisted their new reality.

Dr. Katz certainly agreed with the diagnosis of dementia. Most of the residents were diagnosed with Dementia of the Alzheimer's

Type. Dr. Katz had observed the tragic, relentless progression of memory loss, language impairment, disorientation, loss of abstract thinking ability and overall functioning. By the time they got admitted to this special needs dementia unit, many patients could no longer recognize their spouses or children, utter a coherent sentence, find their way to their rooms down the corridor or use a fork. Most were incontinent and incapable of meeting their most basic needs such as eating or dressing.

In Phillip's case the progression had been a bit "patchy" prior to his admission to the nursing home. He had functioned quite well in some areas, including speech until very recently, but had been quite impaired in other areas such as memory and orientation. This suggested to Dr. Katz that his dementia might have a vascular origin—perhaps the result of multiple mini strokes affecting various areas of his brain in a somewhat random manner rather than the widespread neuron destruction due to the pathological plaques and tangles of Alzheimer's Disease. His tendency to become more confused and anxious as evening approached was referred to as "sundowning" and most likely related at least partly to accumulating fatigue, dimming light and a distorted circadian rhythm. He had struggled with horrible memories of his captivity in WWII, and did exhibit some symptoms of Posttraumatic Stress Disorder such as occasional nightmares and intrusive thoughts, but not full-blown PTSD. His fear that he had again fallen into captivity was likely due to his disorientation and difficulty coming up with a better explanation for feeling stuck in his new and unpleasant surroundings. His agitation seemed perfectly natural to Dr. Katz. How frustrating it must be to be unsure where one is, how one got there, and to sense the loss of one's capacities, the state of powerlessness and overwhelming confusion.

Dr. Katz was frustrated in turn by the lack of effective medical treatments he could offer. Most medications were of little to no benefit and only caused more confusion and grogginess and more serious side effects. That's why he had such tremendous appreciation for Nurse Pamela's efforts to find a humane, individualized approach to making the residents more at ease. She gave them space when they needed it, searched for activities they actually enjoyed, and sought the right balance of stimulation, so that the residents would be neither bored nor overwhelmed. She was criticized by some for disorienting Phillip by talking about WWII, but her approach seemed to fit right in with his own distorted sense of time and most tellingly, it had worked. Phillip's rage had passed. He seemed comfortable for the most part and even appeared to enjoy a moment here and there, which was as good as it got on the dementia unit.

ABOUT THE AUTHOR

Dr. Steve Sobel is a graduate of Tel Aviv Medical School. He completed his psychiatry residency and research fellowship at Hillside-Long Island Jewish Medical Center in NY. He is Clinical Assistant Professor of Psychiatry at the University of Vermont College of Medicine and Medical Director at Northwestern Counseling and Support Services in St. Albans, VT.